Do I Really NEED a Publisher?

I Can Do This By Myself!

Written and Illustrated

by

Johnnie W. Lewis

Marietta, GA USA

This book is by no means the only resource you should use in trying to get your book published. I've ambled around the publishing world for years to get to this point, so I hope this book helps you to "bypass" most of the inefficiency that I've encountered over the past several years.

Johnnie W. Lewis

Lewis, Johnnie W.
    do I really need a publisher? i can do this by myself!

ISBN 978-1500791339

_____

For information regarding permission, write to:
Franklin Wright enterprises
1860 Sandy Plains Rd.
Suite 204 - 150
Marietta, GA 30066
info@acloudproductions / www.acloudproductions.com

Text copyright ©2014 by Johnnie Wright Lewis
Illustrations copyright © 2014 by Johnnie Wright Lewis
Cover art and design by Johnnie Wright Lewis
Published by Franklin Wright Enterprises

Printed by U.S.A.

TABLE OF CONTENTS

INTRODUCTION

OK, let's publish a book!

Believe it or not, writing your book is *usually* the easy part. And it's the "getting it published" part that generally stops people from becoming authors. So, in spite of that statement, I'm including general information about writing in this book, in addition to information on publishing. Whether you want your book in ebook or paperback or hardback does not matter. You can STILL do the publishing part yourself!! Even though I'll give explanations for and about "real" publishers, what we're really going to focus on in this book is SELF-Publishing. Publishing your materials yourself!

Publishing anything (getting the information out of your head and into someone else's) is going to cost someone time, energy, and money (TEM). Whether that TEM is yours or not is strictly up to you.

If you have all three (TEM), you can publish on your own and pray for Divine assistance to get your book noticed by people who want to buy it.
Even though self-publishing will cost you TEM, it's STILL a more guaranteed route to becoming a published author.

As I teach elementary and middle school students in my *You Can Be An Author, Too!* seminars, it takes three things to become an author:

> **IDEA -** You need an IDEA of what you want others to know about, that you can express, whether that expression is in words, pictures, or song. You need an idea. Whether that idea comes from within your own brain or someone else's is not the point. You have to have an *idea* that you want to express to others.

EXPRESS - And that's the next step in becoming a published author. You have to be able to EXPRESS that IDEA in some form that will get that idea "out of your brain" and "into" someone else's brain. Until we, as a species, are able to get our points across to others by mental telepathy, we have to use some external method of *expressing* our ideas so others can absorb them. Most authors use words, written or typed, on paper to express their thoughts. Some use pictures. Author Alexandra Day uses words on only 2+ pages in her children's books, in the "Carl" series; the rest of the expression of her stories are in paintings. Some authors are storytellers via songs. Country singer Don Williams tells wonderful stories, in his songs, painting vivid pictures of his stories in our minds.

SHARE - And that's the next step in becoming a published author. The last step is to SHARE your words with others, in some format, that others can access, whether that format is verbal, written, in pictures, or song. If you keep the words to yourself, it's a diary, not a book. The diary in which Anne Frank wrote her secret thoughts was simply a book of her thoughts, never meant for others to see. But, her death and her father *finding* her diary opened the door to letting the rest of the world *feel* the mind of a young teenaged Jew in the World War II era, one who was just "coming of age" and was just learning about herself and life. Had her father hid her diary, the world would have lost a great insight into the mind of a young girl, struggling to "learn how to live."

Now that you know what's needed to get your book *written*, let's focus on getting it *published*. So, you can take that IDEA you have, that you have EXPRESSED in so many words or pictures, and SHARE it with others! So, you can take your place among the AUTHORS of the world!!

This book is a handbook to getting your "book" into tangible form. It is NOT the "end all" to getting your book published, merely a short-cut from my brain to yours. In fact, I will refer you to many other books and e-magazine articles that will help you in your quest to becoming a published author; whether or not you read those books is up to you. But I have learned one thing over the years since I began this journey — shortcuts taken now will only cost more time later. Example: Initially I tried to by-pass the instructions for putting a book on Amazon, and I just jumped right in and flailed around. When my book "didn't work" on Kindle, I had to go back, delete it from the online store, and figure out what I did wrong. Took twice as long as it would have to get a viable product online than if I had I read the directions in the first place!

Everything is written here in First Person Voice, as if I'm writing this to you, as if you were the only person who will receive this information. That makes it more personal for you and easier for me than trying to remember how to write in Third Person! And I don't always write in "correct" or "proper" grammar. Trust me, I KNOW proper grammar, but I use improper words "for effect," so they will "affect" your own writing and understanding. I try to write like people SPEAK, so they'll understand better. That means I include contractions and "AIN'T" when I'm trying to "get your attention"!! And the bold, italicized words/phrases are defined for you in the Glossary.

I have spent the better part of 10 years amassing the information in this book. For the most part, I've run across this information through trial and error. Try out a method and, if that didn't work, throw that method out and try something new. For the most part, I will tell you how I did it, and whether I succeeded by using a particular method. If using that method did not work for me, but I think it might work for others, I'll let you know that, too.

There are several "prompts" that I will use to get your attention.

One "*" asterisk means "take note of this."
Two "**" means "plan on using this thought or idea."
Three "***" means "you BETTER take note of this idea."
Four "****" means "only D- - - fools ignore this warning."

FAIR WARNING: I am a humorist, pragmatist, and realist, so please don't be "put off" by my apparently "light" banter. The INFORMATION contained within is what is important, not my method of transmitting that information. I try to tell important things with my tongue firmly planted in my cheek. That way, when the medicine goes down and I did NOT take a spoonful of sugar with it, it doesn't taste very badly!!

Johnnie W. Lewis

PREFACE

STEP 1: Get yourself an email address, separate from your personal address, and have _all_ Publishing and Business information sent to that. Don't cross the streams between the two addresses.

STEP 2: Read the rest of this book. Sounds silly I know, but I thought I better tell you the one forgotten item (email address) before I forgot it!

Repeating the Table of Contents, I have divided this book into three sections, in which I will give you caveats about traditional publishing and information about self-publishing:

Follow these instructions for your first published book, which will probably be an ebook. When you decide to publish one in tangible, physical form (printed or audio), you'll have to set up your book for size before you do anything else, then type the book in that size "paper."

Writing an ebook ASSUMES that you'll be writing this book on a computer, rather than a typewriter. If you don't HAVE a computer, typing on a typewriter will limit your manuscript, called MS hereafter, to brick-and-mortar-publishers (b-a-m-p, hereafter) for hardback or paperback printing. **NOBODY will accept a manuscript these days written in longhand or manuscripts printed on a dot matrix printer.

If you don't have access to a computer, consider spending enough time on enough days to retype the entire finished document on a computer at a public library somewhere or use someone else's computer, saving the MS to a thumb dri-ve (or jazz drive or memory stick or whatever you want to call it), in several different formats (*.doc, docx, .pdf, .txt, .pages,* etc.), for use later when you need to attach it to an email to submit it to someone OR to transmit it to a marketplace (more later).

You have to be able to change the formatting on your docu-ment, hence the need for a computer. EBooks (for Kindles, Nooks and other e-readers), for the most part, should not have page numbers, because the text has to be able to "flow" if the reader wants to change the size of the font. Therefore, your ebook formatting will have to be a different file than your formatting for printing purposes, AND for those marketplaces that just want your ebook in *.pdf* format.

So, to make it easier on yourself, save all of your drafts in both ebook AND print formats from the beginning, in the same folder (with the book's title on it) on your computer's desktop. Example: save *jobloegoestotown-ebk* (for your electronic reader versions), *jobloegoestotown-pdf* for .pdf versions, and *jobloegoestotown-pnt* (for your printed ver-sions) in the folder on your desktop named *Jo Bloe Goes to Town*.

You will ultimately want four versions saved:

(1)the original (in case you have to go back to it and make additional files).
(2).*pdf* for print version.
(3).*pdf* for e-readers that will accept that format and for reading on computers.
(4).*doc* and .*docx,* with and without page numbers, and/or headers.

Two separate files, the original and one that can be "played with" (in the folder) on the front end will make it easier to keep them apart. Just remember that every time you make an adjustment or correction to one of the files, you need to make the same adjustment or correction to the other file, too.

~~~~~~~~~~~~~~~~~~~~~~~~

GENERAL INFORMATION ON WRITING YOUR BOOK

For the most part, here are a few steps toward "how to write your book," which is, obviously, the most important part that needs to be accomplished *before* publishing.

Contrary to popular belief, it does you NO GOOD to try and get your book published before you've finished writing it! Fich and ramous (rich and famous) people can do that. Those of us without big bucks or fame behind our names that will grab the public's attention, have to rely on a physical copy of something (such as a MS) to present to someone. So the first steps are:

1. Write your book.
2. Read your book.
3. Edit your book.
4. Read your book.
5. **RE**-write your book.
6. Go back and look at the English Grammar, Punctuation, and Sentence Structure in your book. If it AIN'T right, see step #5.
7. Check into obtaining an ISBN.
8. Think about a cover design (but, unless you're a talented artist, get someone else to design your cover).

After you've completed your MS, print it in draft mode onto cheap paper. Leave at least 1" margins all the way around, so you'll have room to make notes later. Read it yourself first, with an open mind. In fact, **after you "finish" writing your book, put it on the shelf for at least two weeks before you read it again. Distance, in time, helps clear your mind of the "lust" you might feel for seeing your own words on paper and wanting to see them "in a book." I was so excited about hav-ing my first book finished and ready for print, that I didn't do the two-week waiting period. After Step #3 above, I took it to a local printer and ordered 500 copies — without my *NAME* on the cover!

After two weeks, read your book with a red ink pen in your hand. I like Pilot's G2 .07 gel pen for editing (available at WalMart, Office Depot, etc.). After you've used one, you'll understand why! You should note the changes or corrections on your MS in red ink as you read. If you're color blind, make sure you write in the margins so you'll know you need to make those changes that you've noted.

Now, get to editing your book. And it really does NOT do any good to give your "finished" MS to your best friend or sister to read for you (for editing) unless that friend or sister is a qualified editor. I edit books for friends and brothers because I CAN, not because I want to edit YOURS!

But my point is, if you do not feel confident with your use of our language, let someone else edit your book for you. Someone who is good with the language, not someone who will blow smoke up your backside by telling you that "this book is MAHVALOUS!" just because you wrote it. Admittedly, I've written 24 books so far (with about a dozen more in my head!), and I STILL find errors or passages that would have been better expressed, if I had used a different editor than myself. Getting a fresh mind to read your book for you is sometimes helpful!

After you've transferred your changes/corrections to your MS in the computer, **RE**-read your book. If it is NOT the magnum opus you thought it would be, PLEASE don't be so attached to what you've written that you refuse to trash it and start again! Several of Ernest Hemingway's books would have been better, in my opinion, if they had been thrown out and he had begun again. But someone was always blowing smoke up his backside instead of telling him that the book STINKED, STANK, or STUNK!

It's OK to use incorrect grammar, sentence structure, etc. if you're writing a novel and what you're writing is in the vernacular of the peasantry. But, if you're writing a technical manual explaining how to install an engine in a tractor, make sure that NO MISTAKES could be made in the installation of the engine because of a mistake in your grammar or sentence structure! The farmer would not appreciate a tractor that *fills in* the dirt, rather than *plows it up*!

***I know this may not sound like an important point at this point, but it is!! You NEED to pay attention to the placement of pages in your future book. ALL new headings need to start on the facing page (the one on the right), never on the left page. In other words, all new headings (Table of Contents, Glossary, Index, Dedication, Preface, Chapter 1, etc.) start on the right/facing page. Period. End of statement. So when you edit your book on your computer, make sure that you count correctly so that all new heading pages start on the right side. Those will always be the ODD numbered pages. Just remember, even numbered pages on the left, odd numbered pages on the right.

Once your MS is PERFECT, save it (see Preface). Save it in a half-dozen different formats, all in the same folder, (1)so you won't have to go back and save it in one of those formats later and (2)so you can find them easily. Personally, I create a folder with the book's title on it and place it on the desktop (front screen of the computer) for the duration of time that I'm actively working on it, from active writing to published and done. That way, it's VERY easy to find every format I've saved the book in, every picture or map or drawing that is connected to the book, all in the same place.

Saving your MS is the overlap between "Writing Your Book" and "Publishing Your Book." It may seem redundant to save it in numerous formats, but doing so will save you time later. You might not USE all of the formats that you save it in (in which case, *after* publication, you can delete those unneeded formats from your desktop folder), but since it costs nothing extra, except hard drive space right now, save your future time now by saving the MS in different formats, so you won't have to go back and do it later.

Now. What did I just say? Save your MS in several different formats. That means, with lots of different "extensions" or the letters AFTER the "dot," like JOEBLOESBOOK.*doc* or *.docx* or *.txt* or *.pages* or *.pdf* or *.epub*. MOST people have access to Microsoft-based computers, so MOST people will want to save their documents in *.doc, .docx,* or *.pdf* formats. Save the document to all of them in that folder you just created (on the desktop). If you have an Apple-based computer, save it in *.pages*, or export to *.doc, .txt,* and *.pdf* files.

The reason for saving the files in different formats is simple. Different "marketplaces" for your book require that your electronically submitted MS be submitted to "them" (marketplaces) in a specific format (keeping in mind the fact that for Kindle formatting, you need a separate file, one without page numbers). One may want it in *.doc.* One may want it in *.docx.* A third might insist on *.pdf,* but a fourth might want to convert it themselves to *.epub,* in which case they might accept it in *.doc* only. Depends on the marketplace itself. And we will discuss the formats required for each of those different marketplaces later.

A few other things that are required for your published book are (1)a book cover, (2) an ISBN, (3)a barcode (for paperback and hardbacks), and possibly (4)audio/video publishing.

BOOK COVERS

Next to creating the title, the book cover is the most important second step. IF you're an artist or a graphic designer, you might be able to handle creating your book's cover yourself. If NOT, farm out the design to someone who KNOWS what he/she is doing. Simply because it's <u>SO</u> important! The cover design is what your perspective customer sees first. Whether your book is in a bookstore on a shelf, or on Amazon on a computer screen, you HAVE to have something that reaches out and GRABS the shirt of the person with the money, long enough for the title to come into focus. Cover design is that grabber. Then your title has to hold Ms./Mr. Moneybags long enough to get her/him interested in reading the "*elevator speech*" on the back of the book. THEN the prospective purchaser looks at the price.

So. Your cover design is important.

But other than doing the cover yourself, or hiring an expert at an unknown cost, there is another way. Bid it out!

www.fiverr.com (yes, that IS two "r"s!) is a website that is a "jobs wanted" place for people who will do almost any online job for you. SOME of those freelancers will do jobs for you for as little as $5.00 and up. You do have to sign up and sign in (free) on the site, but after that, it's up to you to decide which of the advertisers you might want to try. The price goes up from $5, depending on (1)how much sooner than that person's posted "normal" time-turnaround you want the end product and (2)whether or not you "add" anything to his/her normal amount of work for the requested job. Just be careful. The "norm" may not be sufficient for your job and to add anything may cost more than you had planned. See Appendix I for additional cover design possibilities.

OK, that handles what and how, now let's address formats and sizes.

The "paper" for the book pages need to take into consideration the margins around the verbiage, just as when writing on an 81/2" x 11" sheet of paper. For a book with a finished size of 7" x 10", you can't make the "paper size" for your MS 7" x 10". Maybe 6" x 9" "paper size," but not the full size of the finished book. Or if your word processing program will allow it, set the paper size for 7" x 10" with a 1/2" margin all the way around.

If you are printing or having a paperback book printed for you, you need a book cover that is two widths plus a spine width wide and one length tall. Hardbacks and ebooks need different sizes.

*Ex. 1: A 6" x 9" paperback with 35 pages, will need a cover that is 12.25" wide by 9" high. (6" + 6" + .25" [width] x 9" [length])
*Ex. 2: A 7" x 10" hardback book, with 100 pages, will need a cover that is 15.5" wide by 11.5" high. (7" + 7" + 2" x 11.5") The 2" and 11.5" are more than on a paperback. Spine width might by .5", but the extra 1.5" of width is needed for the overlap pasting of the cover around the width edges of the hardback book, .75" on each end. Height or length of the book will be 10", but the extra inch and a half of the 11.5" will be used to fold over the top and bottom of the book, .75" on each. (See drawing on Appendix I.)
*Ex. 3: An ebook will only need a picture of the cover that will be reduced by "the system" (in your chosen marketplace's system) to a thumbnail picture to be seen online next to the description of your book. **Make sure you put a 1-2 point wide border around your ebook cover and save that picture to a .jpg file. Most marketplaces won't take the ebook cover uploaded in any other format than .jpg.

Audio/visual covers. Two separate issues here. Should you record your own audio/visual recording and create your own cover with that recording or hire someone else to record the audio CD or visual DVD and then someone to create the cover for you? That's one issue. OR should you hire someone to record the book for you and turn it over to someone else to create the cover?

Few people will want to record their books on CD or DVD. BUT, if you have a book that is instructive as some of mine are, you may need a way of recording it professionally. See Appendix III for suggestions on recording your book.

Then there is the problem of duplicating your recordings that is cheap and easy. After you have one original, what are you going to do about getting copies of that CD/DVD made and getting those copies into the hands of your customers? Yes, look on Google for A/V recording companies. But, the one that I've used numerous times, for audio AND video recording duplication is Kunaki. They will produce for you a DVD, in the regular DVD case, wrapped in plastic for a maximum of $1.75 each (CDs are even cheaper, in a jewel case, wrapped). You can't beat that with a stick!! The only two glitches to using them are (1)Kunaki is a BARE BONES company that produces everything by mechanization ONLY and won't answer phones and rarely answers emails. What you send them is what you'll get. If there are any mistakes on the file or cover art that you sent, it will be on the proof. And (2)they only accept transmissions of files from Windows-based computers. If you have an Apple computer as I do, you need to borrow someone's Windows computer for the 10 to 12 hours that it will take to transmit your less than 2-hour file (they can produce CDs/DVDs longer than two hours, but anything over two hours would have to on a separate file and DVD and would be treated as such, i.e., Volume 1 and Volume 2. The instructions are a little blatant and "direct," but this is a company that normally does duplication *en masse* "for the industry." They're being "kind" to let us "lowlifes" (non-professionals) into their fold. Check them out at kunaki.com.

ISBNs & Barcodes

An ISBN (International Standard Book Number) is required, along with an encoded barcode, for any physical book that is sold in a store, to be placed in a library, etc. *If you, personally, are selling it or giving it away at a convention, speech, etc., you probably won't need one, but if you want to be able to keep up with high volume inventory, get one.* Pick up any book and look on the back of the book, bottom right or left and read the number under the bar code. This number is the Library of Congress's (LOC) baby and is its way of keeping up with all the books published in the USA and Australia. Originally a 10-digit number (my older books still have a 10-digit number), but all ISBNs issued these days have 13 digits.

The LOC has given only one company the right and responsibility to issue ISBNs, so don't be fooled. Only **BOWKER.com** can issue/sell viable ISBNs. Yes, other companies will issue them, but it's only because they *bought* the numbers in bulk from Bowker and are re-selling them to you, then transferring the number from their name to yours.

Bowker sells ISBNs for $125 for 1, $295 for 10, $575 for 100, or $1,000 for 1,000 numbers. The more numbers you buy, the cheaper they are individually. Or you can buy an ISBN and a barcode together, at $150 for 1 ISBN + 1 Barcode Combo. Or for $320, you can buy 10 ISBNs + 1 Barcode Combo. But if you are a small publisher or single book author, do you really need 1,000 ISBNs? Other companies are buying the numbers in bulk (because you can't afford to) and reselling them to you at a more-than-you-should-have-to-pay,-but less-than-you-*could*-have-paid price. They'll buy the numbers in 1000 unit lots, then sell them off for less than $125. You save money, they make a TON of money. Example: **isbn-us.com** will sell you a single ISBN for $55, which includes a barcode. They make $54 on the ISBN and the barcode is generated by a software program that they purchased for a one-time fee. Ex. #2: Create Space, printing arm of Amazon, GIVES an ISBN to anyone who publishes a book through them, although the ISBN remains in Create Space's name. Trade-offs…

Check out this link to get your most up-to-date information on buying ISBNs. **https://www.myidentifiers.com/Get-your-isbn-now**. You'll also need a barcode, but more on that in a minute.

NOW. Having said all of that about buying ISBNs, here's a little bit of relief. Ebooks don't have to have an ISBN. It's perfectly alright to have one, but it's not required, usually because people sell their ebooks on their own websites.

If you're selling paperback or hardback copies of your books, you will need an ISBN if you want to sell your books at any portal other than your own website. From your own website, you don't need one, period, because the purpose of an ISBN is to make tracking and inventory purposes easier by mechanizing them. But, if others are selling your books for you, they will usually require that you have one, usually for any of the three formats (ebook, paper, and hardback). And if you combine the books together in any sort of collection, a separate ISBN is required for each collection.

Example:
>   Volume XYZ — gets one ISBN in paperback.
>   Volume XYZ — gets a different ISBN in hardback.
>   Volume XYZ — gets a separate ISBN for a set of Volume XYZ1 and Volume XYZ2 and Volume XYZ3 combined (in paperback, and a different ISBN again for all three books in hardback).
>   Volume XYZ — gets a different ISBN for an audio recording of it.

SO. It is possible for you to use as many as 4-6 ISBNs for a single book in its different formats and in different combinations with other books.

That means that your initial investment in ISBNs for printed paperback books is going to be $295.00, right? NOPE! Gotta better way to go. AMAZON!! As I said, Amazon's paperback printing arm of the company is called Create Space. Have your book printed through CS and they will assign an ISBN, if you choose to let it be listed in the LOC under their name. That may not be the way you want it to be permanently, BUT when you're just starting out as a self-published author, you want to spend as little as possible of your own money. Here's to your first savings!

Once you've gotten your ISBN, whether by purchase or assignment from Create Space, you need a **barcode** that can be scanned at the point of purchase. There are many places to obtain one on the internet, some for a fee, some free. Plug in "barcodes" in the search bar of your search engine to find places to buy a barcode or buy software for printing one. If you were publishing hundreds of books, it would be worth having your own software to create bar codes. But, for onesies - twosies, it's cheaper and easier to get a barcode from a "free" site.

Plugin "free online barcodes" in the search bar and hundreds of sites will appear (Google is the most comprehensive search engine). On any of them, you will need to know what format you want your barcode in. Do you know what EAN, Code 128, Code 13, etc. means? Neither do I!! But some of those sites want you to be able to pick one format over the others. For myself, I just go to a site that gives me a combination barcode (one that includes a separate barcode for the book price, too), for use in the USA as well as Europe. I use: bookow.com/resources.php. You need to save your barcode in 2-3 different additional "formats" — .png, .pdf, and .jpg, if you want it pretty and "camera ready." The *.png* format will save the barcode on a transparent background, so you can use it over any light color. You'll need the *.pdf* for Create Space and other paperback submissions, and the *.jpg* is good for hardback printing.

See Appendix II for samples of a title and copyright (the back of the title page) pages for printed pages (from one of my books). These are different for ebooks, since you don't need most of the information on these pages.

Now that you've written, edited, re-written, re-edited, and saved your MS (you've used your IDEA and EXPRESSED it), it's time to look toward SHARING that IDEA, by publishing your MS.

PUBLISHING YOUR BOOK

There are a dozen different ways to get your books in the hands of the public. And there are advantages and disadvantages to each of the paths (most ways are compared here), whether your book is published by a "brick and mortar" publishing company or you publish it yourself (self-publishing). FOR THE MOST PART, self-publishing is the only way that YOU can maintain control and ownership of your MS. It will cost you more in time and money on the front end as a self-funded publisher, but if your book becomes a best seller, you will reap FAR MORE benefits and remuneration than if someone else published the book for you.

Here's my concept of what being a "Publisher" is. A publisher is the person or entity that takes your writing from MS to published form, whether that form is printed (in soft cover [paperback] or hard cover [hardback]), electronic form (ebook), or auditory recording, along with handling all advertising for the book, all publicity, editing and printing, distribution, sales, and disbursement of funds.

Just because you want to publish your MS yourself does not mean EITHER of the following:

1. Your job will be *easier* than dealing with a b-a-m-p. You will make more money. You will have more exposure, since you have more control over your books.
2. Your job will be *harder* than dealing with a b-a-m-p. You will make less money. You will have less exposure, even though you have more control over your books.

There are no guarantees. Just as there are no guarantees that a b-a-m publisher will do more for you than you can for yourself. But there IS one guarantee with self-publishing. YOU WILL ALWAYS KNOW WHERE IN THE **PIPELINE** YOU ARE, WHEN YOU ARE DOING YOUR OWN PUBLISHING!!

Let's review the I-E-S principles — you need an **Idea**, which you can **Express**, that you finally **Share**, in this case through publishing.

There are innumerable combinations of steps you can take before you see a hard copy (in paper, whether hardback or paperback) or an ebook copy of your book in front of you. The order of many of those steps are determined by what publishing outlet or marketplace and marketing plan you decide to use. We'll touch on as many of those steps, hopefully in the order you will need, as possible, starting with the most used marketing *outlet* in the world and moving to a few of the more obscure.

BRICK AND MORTAR PUBLISHING

AFTER all the hoopla required to finish writing your book, you then have to try to get a (small, medium, or large) brick-and-mortar publisher (b-a-m-p) to publish your book. A b-a-m-p is called such, if they have a physical building, a physical location that people can walk into and talk to a "body." There are numerous steps that you have to go through before publication with a b-a-m-p.

1. **Get the Publisher's attention.** Some publishers won't accept unsolicited MSs from writers. Some will. Get yourself a copy of *Writer's Market,* published by Writer's Digest. It contains all the information on how, where, when and to whom you should send your MS, in addition to what format (electronically) or kind of paper, for "hard copy" submissions. If you can't afford to buy your own copy of the book (they're $20 - $34, but are also available in ebook), most public libraries will have at least one copy, but may not let you check it out. If you use the library's copy, plan on photocopying the pages you need (30-50)

so you can take it home with you, or plan on enough time to sit with the book and write yourself notes on what you need from it. Also, go to www.writersdigest.com and avail yourself of the gazillions of helpful aids for writers on that site.

Agents. Another way to get the publisher's attention is to get a literary agent and let the agent submit your MS to b-a-m-ps for you. Oftentimes, that can be just as hard as submitting the MS yourself, because agents tend to change their "field of interest" as often as they change their underwear. If it says in the book (*Writer's Digest* and whatever other resource you may have found by search-ing the internet under the search keywords "literary agents") that Agent XXX will accept unsolicited MSs on pet care in Bulgaria from unpublished authors, that may have been true *when the book went to press.* But keep in mind that the resource book in your hands was sent to press a MINIMUM of six months (usually 12 months earli-er) before it was delivered to the library or bookstore where you obtained it. A LOT of things can change in six months. A flood or tornado can physically take out the brick-and-mortar building as easily as the mentioned agent can decide that his/her agenting job is not nearly as exciting as watching grass grow in Alaska, leaving you with a book containing information that is no longer correct or relevant.

Just do the best research that you can on picking out a company to send your MS to, keeping in mind the "unso-licited MS" part and the time of year and the minutiae of other details of getting your MS into a book will affect to whom you send it.

Another thought is that once you've picked out the agents or publishers who you think would be most receptive to your genre of book, CALL the agent/publisher/company and ask the person answering the phone if the information you read in the book is still current, including whether or not they still accept unsolicited manuscripts, is the address still the same, and what's the person's NAME now (verify the spelling) to whom you should address your MS. Any and all of these items could have changed since the book was printed.

2. **How much will I make?** Your publisher is in the business to make money for him/itself primarily, and maybe for you. He/she/they do that by selling your book for you. With that in mind, the publisher wears MANY hats. The company is, once they accept your MS and decide to publish it, responsible for ALL of the editing, marketing, book design, publicity, printing, shipping, and distribution of your book. For all those services, the company (which also includes the bookstore that sells your book) will KEEP up to 93% of every dollar that your book makes. THAT'S where you have to ask yourself "Is it worth it to make ONLY 7 cents from every dollar on my book?" Your choice. See the information in the Self-Publishing Section.

3. **What can I do to make a greater percentage of every sales dollar from this publisher?** Get on TV and get famous. Publishers *love* to publish for the fich and ramous, because it cuts down on their need for publicity expenditures and increases the chances that MANY people will buy your book. But if you aren't already famous, don't count on the company doing back handsprings to get in line to sign you up. If you have a PhD behind your name, your chances are greater of getting your book on the *History of Glass* published. But if you DON'T have that PhD, good luck getting the attention that your book on *Raising Rabbits in Rangoon* deserves.

Honestly, I'm not being silly. I'm just being brutally honest about how HAAARRRDDD it is (1)to get your foot in the door of a b-a-m-p, (2)to get your book published, and (3)to get on TV and radio to increase your book sales, unless you already have gold (or fame or the greatest invention since sliced bread) in your pockets. HENCE, the urge for writers to publish their works themselves. NOW. In spite of the glaring realities of getting your book published by a "company," here are the REAL realities.

The *Pipeline* (the length of time from the time you submit your MS until your book is selling in the bookstores) is changeable, long, circuitous, changeable, impressionable, changeable, and changeable. And did I mention changeable? For the most part, with the b-a-m-p, you submit your MS and wait. And wait. And wait. *IF* your MS is accepted for publication. If not, you'll get the MS back (if you sent a SASE with it) within 1-6 months or, if you're lucky, you might get a short note that says, in effect, "Thanks, but no thanks." For the most part, here's what "they" (the people at the "Publisher") are doing while you're "sitting on your thumbs," waiting for an answer about your submitted MS:

1. MS sits in a "*slushpile*" for 1-6 months before someone decides to open the envelope. Even so, always send your MS, solicited or unsolicited, with a SASE enclosed (Self-Addressed Stamped Envelope). And when they send it back, it'll be mangled and man-handled, but at least YOU can destroy it and it won't be sitting around in someone's office for someone else possibly to steal it and plagiarize it. OR, if you are lucky and they agreed to accept it electronically, about the same period of time will pass before someone opens your "file" to look at the MS for the first time. MS is then passed to a "reader" who may work for the company or may be an outside contracted person, and who is assigned to read the MS and make a suggestion on the book based on what he/she decides about the book, i.e., over-used subject, great writing, suggest

rewrites; great subject and plot, poor writing, suggest rewrites; trite subject, poor writing, send it home.

2. IF your MS is accepted for further review, it is sent to the first editor, who decides whether or not the company will publish your book. And there's the rub. One-two people's decisions on whether or not THAT company can make money off your book!! You should notice that I said "company can make money off your book." I didn't say that they decided that everyone needs to READ your book for the betterment of mankind or something, I said "can they make money from publishing it." That's what is driving them. Money. NOT whether or not your book contains the cure for cancer or the *greatest* new energy source. Like any good fiscal company, they are motivated by the possibility of making money. Nothing else. If the MS GETS that far, here are the next steps:

3. MS to another editor for editing.

4. MS to re-editing.

5. MS to you for rewrites.

6. MS to editor for re-re-editing.

7. Cover design people are "brought on board" (now or sooner) to begin the design of the book cover. If it's a romance novel, Fabio's schedule is checked to determine whether or not he's available for modeling for photos. Any old girl will do, but Fabio is a ***must*** as the male on the front cover. (snicker, snicker)

8. If the MS doesn't need a second or third re-write, MS is sent to a committee to schedule production. In that committee, all of the other "players" will come together over croissants and latte (remember, they need "expenses" to justify only giving you a certain amount!) to discuss their various roles in the "release" of the book.

   - Cover design group will give their updates (is the artist, who is rendering Fabio's best photo into an oil-on-canvas, on schedule?).

   - The production group will be told to put the book into the "line-up" for printing, after the decision is made as to what date the release will be. After printing, will the book be **permabound** (glued and smashed tightly in a vise, _if_ it's under 150 pages) or **saddle-stitched** (pages SEWN or STAPLED together and cover glued on separately)? Small, thin pamphlets or booklets may be stapled togeth-er in the crease (also called saddle-stitched), but most smaller books and paperbacks are permabound. Most larger books and hardbacks are saddle-stitched (sewn through the thickness of the book). Except thick paper-backs, which are usually permabound.

- The publicity department will be told to begin contacting the various media outlets with news of the upcoming re-lease and start arranging public events for the author to attend.
- "Oh, and will someone PLEASE contact Johnnie, so she'll quit calling us, and let her know that we're on schedule to release her book in Judember?"

9. Depending on the photographer/artist's schedule, it could take 2-4 months for the cover art to be completed.
10. Depending on the production department's schedule, it could take 3-5 months for copies of the book to be printed. The cover art has to be completed before printing begins, so the cover can be printed simultaneously and bound to-gether with the pages.
11. Depending on the publicity department's schedule and the schedule of the various media outlets, it could take 2 weeks to 5 months to get the author on TV/radio shows/programs. Usually, the TV/radio shows aren't scheduled until a very few DAYS before delivery to the bookstores, so that the two coincide. You don't want publicity to start TOO soon (more than 2 weeks) before the actual book is released or people will forget about the book by the time it's released. OR for the publicity to come after release, because it's not making any money for you _or_ the others whose livelihood depends on sales of your books, if it's sitting on the "New Releases" shelf, but no one's heard of it yet. People won't buy a "pig in a poke." Being on the

radio *within the same week* as the release of the book is good.

12. Continual publicity is good. After release of the book, and sales figures start coming in, it is still good to be on radio and TV shows to continue to promote the book. Especially if it is selling well. New York Times Bestseller lists are compiled from bookstore sales — ONLY. And best-selling authors are asked BACK on TV shows. But wannabe best-selling authors AIN'T.

13. Once the book is on the shelves, the publisher wants to wash hands and move on to another book. Marketing and Publicity in the months/years after the initial sales wane is UP TO YOU!

****In order to keep your book in the public's eyes, you need to keep YOU in the public's eyes. Make sure that all newspaper and radio/TV statements about you reference your status as "author of the great new book, *Blah Blah Blah Blah*." The best publicity you can give your book in the months/years after publication is to keep you and the book in the public's eye. Write a sequel.

Depending on whether or not the above schedules can/will overlap, your book could be on the shelves (through a large publisher) in 12-18 months. If it's through a medium to small publisher, it could be 6-12 months. AFTER you've already spent 1-101 months saying grace over your MS.

What I didn't mention was remuneration. IF, and that's a big IF, you have a well-known name and are writing on a spectacular subject, you MIGHT get an advance on the royalties from sales. If you aren't a former President of the United States, you not only won't get an advance, but you will have to wait up to a year to receive even the first few cents from your book. B-a-m-p's usually disburse monies only twice a year, six months in arrears of when the money was earned. Example: Publisher PQR releases your book in March. It has great sales for 3 months, then the sales taper off. But you won't receive your money at their half-year fiscal point (if it's in June), you will receive your money, for March - May sales in December, before their end-of-year closing or in January after EOY closing. Remember, they're in business to make money. Not to give YOU money.

Advances on royalties that you MIGHT have received as the production process began are USUALLY taken out of that first royalty check, meaning you might or might not receive a royalty check. Unless their agreement with you is that YOU receive the advance because of WHO you are and you are NOT required to pay it back. Depends on the contract you signed.

So. That's the OPTIMISM of getting your book published by a b-a-m-p. Now, let's look at publishing your own work!

SELF-PUBLISHING

SUPPLIES/EQUIPMENT NEEDED TO BECOME A SELF-PUBLISHER:
* Computer, with either Windows or Apple operating system (instructions here will be for both, for the most part). Sure, you can use a typewriter, but you still need a computer, even if it's borrowed, to send your submissions to your marketplaces either by email or to upload your MS to a publisher or agent.
* Desktop Printer, set on draft for corrections, but that can print "best" for submissions to publishers if you still want to try the B-A-M-P route. If you can get a publisher or agent to accept your MS, they will NOT accept dot matrix printings.
* Lots of cheap paper, for printing draft copies for corrections/ changes.

* A ream or so of good paper, say 28# to 32# weight, for printing out letters or sample copies of the MS for submission to magazines and other print "marketplaces."
* Expendable MONEY, that won't take the bread out of your children's mouths. Believe it or not, you WILL need to spend some of your own money in this endeavor.

Publishing your own works means that you are taking over ALL of the roles of a publisher mentioned earlier. You must BE the book's editor or FIND one who will edit the book for you for free or for a price you can afford to pay. Yes, because as a self-publisher you don't have the B-A-M-P's money bags behind you, the $$ to do all the things the B-A-M-P does has to come from somewhere. And where better than from the person who stands to GAIN the most from the sale of your book? YOU! YOU have to find someone to design your book cover, handle all the computer glitches, pay for publicity, buy advertisements, contact the appropriate TV, radio stations, and newspapers, and convince them to accept you on a show to talk about your book.

It means that you are putting up the money to get your MS into print. You have to handle the printing of your books, whether you print them yourself OR find a third-party printer who will print your books for you at a price you can afford OR find a commercial printer (not the kind that sits on your desk) who will handle "***print on demand***" orders for your customers. YOU have to arrange for your book all of the marketing and publicity and displays and speeches, ta da, ta da, ta da, ad enaseum. Having to do all the work yourself gives you a *slight* inkling of why the brick-and-mortar publisher feels that he/she/they DESERVE to keep 88% - 93% of every dollar that YOUR book might bring into their company.

From ALL of this work, you glean the satisfaction of knowing everything about the book publishing process, and knowing that everything that COULD be done to get your book in front of the public's eyes has been done. Everything except getting the public to purchase your book. That will come with time, exposure, the public's familiarity with your name and the name of your book, and continual familiarity with the REASON why the public NEEDS your book.

And once again, the ugly serpent of remuneration rears its head. HOW MUCH WILL I MAKE? That, of course, depends on the numbers of sales you make. Get a copy of John Locke's ebook, *How I Sold 1 Million eBooks in 5 Months!* on Amazon for $2.99. Once you get past the fluff, he does have a few VERY GOOD tips on what to do to boost your sales. But the answer to the question posed is a question: Will you have a better chance of making money from a b-a-m-p, selling your magnum opus for $24.95 each, in hardback, or for 9.95 in paperback on Amazon, Barnes & Noble, etc.? Let's compare the best and worst case scenarios.

- $24.95 x 12% (IF you're someone special and can command that kind of a percentage from a publisher; if not, you'll get 7%) = $2.99 per book royalty paid to you, 7 months to a year from now.
- $12.95 x 35% (the LEAST you would get from Amazon for a book sold in India) = $4.53 per book royalty paid to you, at the end of next month.

Now, if you are Elvis recently returned from the dead and have written your memoirs (in which case *I* want to be the first in line for an autograph!!!), you might get 12% and have millions of sales at $24.95 per sale. And on the other hand, if you are Joe Bloe, the local Schmo, NOBODY will pay $24.95 to read your book about turning concrete into GOLD (that would equal $0.00 in sales). But if you sell your ebook on concrete alchemy for $0.99 on Amazon, hundreds or even thousands of people are more willing to say "*enh*, it's only

99¢, that's no biggy! Let's see what he's got." And at 35% royalty (or 70%, if you don't care about selling in India or Japan or Mexico), your royalty would be 35¢ or 70¢ per ebook download, times 10,000 downloads equals $10,500 or $21,000. In other words, you're gambling. Will you make more money from selling a few expensive books for a small percentage or selling more books cheaply for a larger percentage? Which do you think gives you a better shot at seeing some cold, hard cash? Self-publishing, right!! Oh, give the man a ciGAR!!

So. Are you STILL hot-to-trot toward your goal of publishing your book yourself? EXCELLENT!! Let's get started. I LIKE dealing with people who are just as nutty as I am!!

There are MANY questions or situations that need to be posed by a new self-publisher. Your answers to these questions/statements will help you determine your path through the publishing maze, on any marketplace site, but on Amazon in particular, where indicated. And at the beginning of each new paragraph or section, I'll put separate acronyms for the type of cover format those instructions are for — **E** (ebook), **P** (paperback), **H** (hardback) or combinations of the three. The reason I'm not just putting a section for each of the three by itself is because most of the information overlaps to two or three book covers or formats, not just one.

1. **P,H.** Deciding whether or not a particular MS could and should be published to the world is an important question you have to ask yourself. Just because YOU want to see it in print does NOT mean that anyone else would PAY you for it to be in print. Fine line there. If you *really* want to see your book in print and don't care if anyone else buys it, you need to look for a Vanity Press. They don't CARE if anyone ever buys your book. Their focus is to put your book into print and charge you for that privilege. The dif-

ference is in whether or not you have to pay the company for their services "up front" or they take their money as a percentage of your sales. Payment up front makes it a Vanity Press. Percentages taken from your sales after printing makes it Self-Publishing. See Appendix V for suggested Vanity Presses. But remember to *caveat emptor* ("let the buyer beware").

2. **E,P,H.** Editing or having the MS edited so that it works appropriately for the genre the book is in AND reflects the voice in the book. This is one of those things that should go in the "…Writing Your Book" section, but it bears repeating here. If it's written in third person voice, the omnipotent voice SHOULD use correct English grammar, unless when, on occasion, the voice is trying to gain the reader's attention, to illustrate a point, or show the vernacular of the speaker. And sometimes even then, the words used by a first person speaker will revert to correct English most of the time, but will show the slang in the thoughts occasionally to remind you of his/her origin.

3. **E,P,H.** Formatting the MS so that, when printed on paper, the words don't run to the edge or run OFF the edge of the paper; the font is easy on the eyes; and the typeface or font is large enough to be read easily, but not so large that more paper is required to print the book, reducing your profit margin. Not everyone feels that a *sans serif* typeface is good for the printed word. If you feel it's not "good enough" for your use, use Times New Roman or something similar that doesn't have *extreme* "little feet" that bothers other readers. NOTE: usually a *sans serif* font ("sans" means "without"; so *sans serif* means "*without line*" on the edges of the letter — E] such as Arial"). In other words, either use Times New Roman or Arial.

4. **E.** Format the MS so that, when sold as an ebook, it won't "clog up" and will be easily readable on electronic readers or on a computer in *.pdf* format.

5. **E,P,H.** Arrange publicity with radio and TV stations, internet radio, newspapers, libraries, schools (if your book is

meant for them), book stores, etc., etc., etc. That means posters to put in windows, interviews for radio, good clothes for TV (that don't look wrinkled [unbutton your jacket], frumpy, too small, too large, etc. as you are sitting), a happy face and warm smile for ANYONE who asks you about your books. That includes a 15-20 second *"elevator speech."* *****NEVER, when asked what your book is about, NEVER give someone the entire plot of the book.** It'll bore them, tick them off, and make it hard for them to WANT to read it, even if they bought it. Give them the nuts and bolts and THAT'S ALL!! "It is the story of a young woman who grew up in an orphanage and when selected as a governess for an unknown family, finds her life in peril almost from the beginning. There is mystery, lust, greed, jealousy, admiration and happiness for her in the end." Only if someone specifically asks for the plot should you go into it! (Can you see the $$ mounting up to get your book into print?)

6. **P,H.** If you plan on printed copies of your book, invest in 25+ copies so you will have a few to give away as "review copies" and for the TV personalities who interview you. That's the "gracious" way to go through an interview process.

7. **E.** If you plan on having your book only available as an ebook, have a plan in place for "gifting" your interviewer with a copy of your ebook. That means, have a place on your website where your "TV contact" can go (make it private so no one else can get to it) to download your *.pdf*. Or, if you have an ecommerce site set up, create a "coupon code" that makes it easy for your "contact" to obtain your *.pdf* without charge.

8. **E,P,H.** There are other ebook marketplaces, but some require that you "join" them and pay a fee for your "membership." DON'T DO IT, regardless of what they promise you in terms of sales of your book. It's a rip-off!

NOTE: If you don't have access to a Kindle so you can check to see what your book looks like "on screen," you can download a copy of a Kindle Previewer for computers and download your book to the reader to see what it will look like on a real Kindle. Go to this link to get your Kindle Free Previewer App: www.amazon.com/gp/feature.html?docid=1000493771

~~~~~~~~~~~~~~~~~~~~~~~~~~~

Now comes the SHARING part of the "I-E-S" process. "Sharing" your idea with others means that, as a publisher, you are responsible for "dissemination of all informational materials."

Here are a few of the marketplaces that I have tried for placing books and ebooks:

Amazon (amazon.com) *Free sign-up, 35% to 70% royalty*
Apple's iBookstore (www.apple.com/ibooks/) *Free, 70% royalty*
Barnes & Noble (pubit.barnesandnoble.com) *40% - 65% royalty*
Kobo (kobo.com) *Free, 70% - 80% royalty*
Smashwords (smashwords.com) *Free sign-up, 60% - 85% royalty*
Teachers Pay Teachers (teacherspayteachers.com) *Free, 100% royalty*
Pinterest (pinterest.com), *Free*

And other marketplaces that I have NOT tried, but look viable and legitimate:

Google Books Partner (for Sony eReaders)
eBay (ebay.com)
Clickbank (clickbank.com) *$49.95 sign-up, 50% - 90% royalty*
Overdrive (https://marketplace.overdrive.com/Account/Login)
Free-Ebooks-Canada (http://free-ebooks-canada.com/?p=5173)
National Novel Writing Month (http://nanowrimo.org)
Chegg (chegg.com/publishers) for Textbooks
Payhip (https://payhip.com) *Free sign-up, 100% royalty*

Lulu (lulu.com) *Free sign-up, 90% royalty; This one looks good!*
   I may be trying this one soon!!
BookTango (booktango.com) *Free sign-up, 100% royalty*
Book Baby (bookbaby.com) *$99 - $249 sign-up, 100% royalty*
Myebook (myebook.com) *Free sign-up, 90% royalty*
Blurb (blurb.com/ebook) *Free sign-up, 80% royalty*
E-Junkie (e-junkie.com) *$5/mo., 100% royalty*
Tradebit (tradebit.com) *$4.95 sign-up, 70% - 85% royalty*
PayLoadz (payloadz.com) *$14.95/mo, 95% royalty*
PaySpree (payspree.com) *Free sign-up, 90% - 100% royalty*
Click2Sell (click2sell.com) *Free sign-up, 90% - 95% royalty*
Instabuck (instabuck.com) *$4.99/mo, 100% royalty*

AMAZON.COM

Any book you want to publish can be placed for sale on Amazon. It is the largest purveyor of merchandise in the world (in fact, Amazon sells about 60% of the books and ebooks sold on the planet!), with iBooks (iTunes) coming in a distant second (20% of the market), and Barnes & Noble a close third for ebooks (15% of the market). All others add up to the other 5%. In addition to being able to buy almost anything on Amazon, you can sell almost anything (new or slightly used) on their website, too. Just in the category of books alone, there are sub-categories of ebooks, hardbacks, paperbacks, all divisible by dozens of genres, uses and potential "readers."

Because of this inordinate "weighting" on the side of the *size* of Amazon's place in the market, most of this information on self-publishing will be aimed at placing your book on Amazon. And most of what follows is NOT information on how to submit, format, etc. your book to Amazon (most of that's in the ebook I'll refer you to). But most of what follows is warnings or caveats, information gleaned from my experiences (read that "mistakes"), misunderstandings and problems I've had because of the voluminous and convoluted nature of the submission instructions for writers/publishers put out by Amazon.

E,P,H. Say, you have a romance novel. You can place your ebook DIRECTLY on Amazon for sale and they handle the download of your product to your end user, collect the money from the customer and distribute your portion to you. All you have to do is follow their steps. Instructions on that later.

E. The first time I put an ebook on Amazon, it took me a WEEK to digest the instructions so that my book could be read on a Kindle. And that week didn't include the time that I kept falling asleep over that boringly written stuff. I didn't have a Kindle myself at the time, so once I uploaded the MS file, I needed a way to look at the book to be sure that it was readable on a Kindle. NOT! The pictures were in one section and the writing was in another. **Ebooks containing pictures WILL pose a few problems, but they CAN be overcome, so don't panic. Nowadays, I start from a different direction, the process is a lot easier, and the product comes out without a hitch!

E. Placing an ebook on Amazon, with the understanding that 75% of the reading population "out there" will have a Kindle or some other sort of e-reader, means that your book has to conform to Kindle restrictions, i.e., the words become a "fluid environment." The end user might be a 90-year-old lady with bad eyesight and needs the words in very large print. On her Kindle, she can change the font size to accommodate her poor vision, which means that all of the words in your book get bigger and the margins change. For that reason, you can NOT use page numbers for Kindle ebooks, because the page numbers might wind up in the middle of her screen "page," since the pages that you originally "envisioned" aren't the same size anymore. Which means that your book is now many pages LONGER than you originally wrote (but only because the font size is different). Or your purchaser might be a young man whose eyesight is excellent and only needs the font size rather small. Then your book is shorter than you wrote on your computer. So, for submission to Kindle, ebooks should NOT have page numbers, footers, or headers of any sort.

E. I know you'll read this in the Kindle information, but just in case... There are a few things that you can NOT put in *your* version (format) that you save for Kindle: NO page numbers, NO charts, NO tabs (set up paragraph indentions in your document), NO more than two hard returns together. Push all pictures to the left margin and <u>don't</u> anchor them or lock them on the page, so they'll flow with the text. Push all chapter titles, and other parts that are centered on the page, to the left margin. Any of these formatting items will cause your book on Kindle to look spastic and disorganized, ticking off your reads. They CAN ask for their $$ back, you know.

E,P. There are THREE different kinds of publishers on Amazon for you to become: (1)a Kindle publisher through KDP (Kindle Direct Publishing) for providing ebooks for reading on Kindles, (2)a Create Space publisher for providing books in paperback form (hardcover publishing is not available through Amazon at this time), or (3)an Audible publisher for providing books in audio form. When registering as an author, all three forms of publishing require the same login, bank account, and author's biographical information. You just sign-up for that information once and use the same "Author's Info" regardless of the form you want your published book to take be it paperback, hardback or ebook. Go to <u>https://kdp.amazon.com</u> to get started.

E. I'm going to do something here that no responsible author would do — direct you to someone else's book! But truly, without plagiarizing the book by copying it word for word here, how else should I give you the most succinct information on how to submit your ebook in *this* book if that information is already available elsewhere? There really is NO reason for me to repeat everything here that is said on Amazon's site about becoming a publisher with Amazon or about how to "upload" your book to Amazon. Not when there is that excellent ebook I referred to earlier, available for FREE, called *Building Your Book for Kindle*. Go to amazon.com, plug in the name of the book in the search bar and download it to your Kindle or the Kindle Reader on your computer. The ebook, written by Amazon employees, is more or less a shrinky-dinked version of the online submission instructions to would-be authors for submitting ebooks. In much less convoluted and confusing words, I might add. Why they didn't just write the submission instructions for the online instructions, in the same words as are in the ebook *Building Your Book for Kindle* to begin with is beyond me!

So, to repeat and to reinforce. The short and sweet of it is that (1)you won't NEED to purchase an **ISBN** if you publish through Amazon (yes, you still need an ISBN, but you don't need one for publishing an ebook, for publishing through Create Space in paperback, or for an audiobook) because you can obtain it through Amazon, and (2)ALL of the explicit instructions that you need for uploading your book to Amazon are in the ebook *Building Your Book for Kindle* referenced above.

E. ****If you are the author of Children's Books or books that will contain LOTS of pictures or drawings or charts, please take NOTE. Up until recently, any book sent to KDP that contained pictures, *et al*, was a pain in the patootie to format for publication. The reason was simple. Kindles are NOT *.pdf* format friendly, which is about the only way that you can keep pictures on the same page with the words that go with them. HOWSOMEVER, very recently, the rules changed and, after YEARS of my fussing to the higher-ups (and probably a lot of other authors did, too!), there is now a way for Kindle to handle the publishing of documents formatted in *.pdf, .jpg,* and *.txt* formatted pages.

When you login to your "bookshelf" at kdp.amazon.com, just to the right of the "Add New Title" box, there is a "Learn more about…" for learning about publishing children's books, comics, etc. Click on the "learn more" and a whole new world opens up. This link will give you detailed info on formatting your highly illustrated books to be put on Kindle. HOWEVER, the directions don't tell you EVERYTHING needed to get your book on KDP. Almost everything, but the directions leave out the keystone.

The Keystone. Once you've put your book into *.pdf* format, and put the book cover on the *.pdf* file, save the file to a BLANK folder on your desktop. "The system" will not LET you save it to a folder that has something else in it. There will be about six saved files in the formerly blank folder. Only one is the book — the one that has the extension *.mobi.* Now go online to kdp.amazon.com and fill in all of the other info for adding a new title to your "stash." But when you get to the part about adding the interior file or middle part of the book, go to the formerly BLANK folder and look for the file that ends in *.mobi* and click on that one to add. THAT'S the part that the instructions leave out. If you try to add your .pdf file for that book from your desktop or somewhere, you'll get error messages about "*.pdf* files don't work well" in the fluid environment of Kindle-ism.

Now. I know that Amazon tries to push you into signing up your book to the KDP program, but personally, I think you would be better off NOT to sign up for the program, at least not in the beginning. If you want to go back later and sign up, do so, but give your book a chance at being on several different marketplaces in the beginning. KDP (Kindle Direct Publishing) is an EXCLUSIVE posting, so that you literally can NOT publish your book to other marketplaces at the same time that it is on KDP. It SEEMS like a good deal, but the potential for sales in different marketplaces simultaneously is eliminated when you have your book listed exclusively with one marketplace. If it were a "shoe-in" and you were almost guaranteed to make lots of money with that exclusivity, that would be WONDERFUL. But since there is STILL no guarantee of sales just because it's listed on Amazon "only," I say it's not worth the exclusive nature of the deal. At least, not in the beginning.

iBOOKSTORE

The next most visited online bookstore is the iTunes bookstore for Apple. If you do not have access to an Apple computer, just skip this section.

If you have access to an Apple computer, download iBooks Author for free from the Apple iBookstore, then convert your book to that format. iBooks are only accepted in the Apple format and in that format, are only to be sold on the Apple/iTunes bookstore. Talk about exclusivity!

It was quite an undertaking for me to convert *The Five Finger Essay* to an Apple format, since I had never done that type of conversion before, but once it was finished, I was ready to convert more books to that format, until I realized the exclusive nature of the arrangement. It doesn't sell very well in their online bookstore, but at least now I have the knowledge to go about converting other books to that format.

BARNES AND NOBLE

The next most prolifically visited website as a marketplace for selling your book(s) is Barnes and Noble. Register yourself as a publisher at nookpress.com, for ebooks. The instructions are VERY friendly, clear (compared to Amazon), and easy to follow. Enter your publisher login information, read the rest of the NOOK Press Features and read each of the six "features." Then skip on down to read the Nook Press FAQs in the Support Section. You're ready to go!! There is also a "Getting started with NOOK Press" video under Support and a Chat Representative for your questions.

Getting your ebook on B&N (via NOOK Press) is terribly easy and quick. Unfortunately, it's really too bad that, unless people KNOW to look for your book on B&N, that you won't sell as many books on B&N as you will on Amazon. But that is caused by the volume of bodies that come to Amazon as opposed to Barnes & Noble.

If you want to be a publisher that supplies paperback and hardcover books for Barnes and Noble, you must present yourself as a b-a-m-publisher, even down to providing reviews, excerpts, etc. of your book. Go to http://www.barnesandnoble.com/help/cds2.asp?PID=8149 to get started. The requirements are NOT as simple and user-friendly as are the NOOK Press instructions for ebooks. An easier way to get your paperback or hardback book into Barnes & Noble is in Baker and Taylor's catalogs (more information in the Lightning Source Section). That way, when your fans go to B&N and request a copy of your book, B&N can order it.

After you've put your book(s) on amazon.com, bn.com (nookpress.com), and Apple's iBookstore (if you have access to an Apple computer), start searching for websites that will take your book without charging you for the privilege. **Never pay, up front, for "membership" to be on someone's website.**

OTHER MARKETPLACES

There are a couple of marketplaces that I've used that are relatively easy to place your book(s) on, especially if it's to be an ebook. Kobo (.com) and Smashwords (.com) are two where I've placed ebooks and I'm satisfied with their progress. Especially since neither company charges an arm and a leg for their services (like Amazon). And, I might add, both are headquartered in the UK.

Do you remember that I said earlier that you might need to adapt your original version to accommodate your paperback and hardback versions? If you haven't done so before now, save a copy of your book, in which you'll now change a few things. Those changes need to include adding the page number, charts, headers, footers, and anything else that you could NOT put in the version you saved for Kindle. This version will be saved in *.doc* or *.docx* (from *.pages*, export your document to *.doc* or *.docx*) for KOBO Smashwords, and *.pdf* for Create Space.

CREATE SPACE

If you don't want your book in paperback, skip to the next section.

I can't sing the praises of Create Space enough. I use them exclusively to print all paperback books in my list. There are about 24 books on their servers with my name (or a pseudonym) on them, in some level of publication readiness. Their price is more per book than a local printer might be, but they are a Print-On-Demand printer. They print when the order comes in and not before. You don't pay for storage of unsold books. Pay more on the front end, but save on the back end of the publishing cycle.

Create Space (CS), the printing arm of Amazon, has two sets of instructions on how to get your book onto their site, after you've filled out all of the "author" stuff and gotten yourself established with the company. One set of instructions is for "experts" (people who have experienced putting a book on CS before) and another set called "Guided," for Beginners. Choose the Guided button the first time, 'cause believe me you'll need it. Dummy here chose Expert the first time, AS-SUMING (you know what *that* does!) that it meant what level you're at in your WRITING career. Fumbled around for a few days before I gave up and went back to the "Guided" button. The instructions there explain every step, and *guide* you (Duh!) through the maze of information.

Another button you have to click on after you enter the name of your project is the type of project: paperback, Audio CD, MP3, DVD, or Video Download. I can't wait until they will ALSO produce hardback books! Maybe…

CS will "lend you use" of an ISBN for your paperback book, if you so choose, or you may use your own. They will also let you compile financial reports on numbers of books sold, etc.

All of your books will be available for distribution through SEVERAL different markets, so that without your advertising money, your books are still available for sale on sites all over the world.

CS gleans their revenue from you, based on the retail cover price of your book. Their percentages are based on your choice of worldwide distribution or domestic and the price you choose to sell your book. Set up your account with them at createspace.com.

LIGHTNING SOURCE & INGRAMSPARK

If you don't need your book in hardback and aren't interested in your book being in libraries, skip to the next section.

If you're interested in getting your books into public, school and institutional libraries, Lightning Source (LSI, a subsidiary of IngramSpark) is the place to get your hardback books printed. They can produce your book in all formats (ebooks, softcover, hardback, or audio), but I only use them for hardback, and for a very good reason. COSTS. Every book submitted and every format for that book (ebook, paperback, etc.) is charged a separate set-up fee.

Since I have a good source for getting my softcover books printed (Create Space) and equally good source for placing my ebooks (all the marketplaces listed earlier), I don't feel the need to PAY someone to print paperback books or to store ebooks on their servers. Granted, that makes my ebooks almost "invisible" to libraries, but are there that many libraries in the country, yet, that offer ebook readers for rent so you can download ebooks to them? Not really..., not yet anyway. So I don't consider ebooks worth the "processing fee" to get them onto LSI's list. Yet.

On the surface, LSI looks like a *vanity press*, but it's not. B-A-M-Ps send their books to LSI for printing and distribution. Only a few presses in the country (the printers of your books) have the connections that Lightning Source does, as part of their normal operations. Yes, you have to pay THEM to get your book printed, and no, they don't promote your book for you, so in that aspect, it's a vanity press. But vanity presses don't have the access to the catalogs and markets that Lightning Source does. And THAT'S what makes them such a valuable resource.

Yes, they cost more than other companies that produce hardback books in smaller quantities, but here is the benefit that you get for that extra buck spent:

Baker and Taylor.

B&T is the largest distributor of physical and digital books in the world. After publication at Lightning Source, your book's title automatically goes onto their distribution list and into their catalogs, which go to every public, private, and institutional library and bookstore in the country and many overseas. It doesn't go on those lists at most vanity presses because most of them don't have the connections to such catalogs and lists. Those connections alone are worth whatever it costs for publication/printing. You can not just publish your own books, get them printed somewhere, keep your own stockpile, and then "get on" the distribution lists and in the catalogs. You can't "pay" to get on their distribution lists and catalogs, because they won't accept you. And since those lists and catalogs are the ONLY place that libraries and most bookstores order their books from, the media specialists need to see your book in that catalog in order to buy your book. And since there are about 120,100 libraries of all kinds in the country (public, academic, school, special, Armed Forces, and Governmental), it would be a physical impossibility for you to get the name of your book in front of the eyes of every library's purchaser without the title being on some sort of collective list..., such as B&T's catalogs.

What does it cost to get your book published? Well, after you register as a publisher with the company at www.lightning-source.com, you'll be able to get an estimate of how much it will cost to print the book by entering the specifics (number of pages, size of book, color ink or black and white) in the screens that will help you estimate your costs. From that, you can fix the sales price. Then, follow the fairly simple instructions for uploading your electronic file for your hardback book. Each book is a different wholesale price, based on color content, volume, book cover, paper quality, ta da, ta da, ta da. But for the most part, a 150 page, 6"x9" black and white book, full of words and/or black and white drawings would cost about 1/3 what one of my full-color *Flutterbye, the Butterfly* books costs, at about $9 each.

Keep in mind that this company is used to dealing with MA-JOR b-a-m-p publishers as their printer and will brook no stu-pidity on your or my part. Registering one title with them will cost $75, and ALL of YOUR changes/corrections will cost $40 each. That means that if you "accidentally" sent them an in-correct file or sent one with the wrong cover or the wrong margin or wrong typeface, each submission for changes will cost $40. If you goof up, submit your corrected file with ALL of your changes simultaneously.

Yes, if they print something incorrectly, they need to make the change at their expense, and they will. But if it's your correc-tion or change, you'll pay for it. And there is a difference in what you pay for the books (and what your customers will pay when they place orders) between ordering your printed books from them as a wholesaler or a print-on-demand order. Read up on the differences, according to LSI, before you place your order. And they REQUIRE that they send you a PROOF copy, which will cost more than the cover price of the book. But it's worth that price to know that what you have in your hand (the proof) is exactly how every subsequent copy will look.

WEBSITE

I know it seems redundant to have your books on Amazon and to have a website, but there is a really good excuse for that. Your customers. People are sheeple, but it depends on whether their own lead sheep is a website person or one devoted to shopping or Tweeting or Facebooking or wherever their devotions lie.

You at least need to have your name and the name of your book on a website somewhere, along with on other sites that handle materials that are similar to the subject of your book. It doesn't have to be an expensive one or have a whiz-bang name person to create the site for you, but you do need one for the exposure and for the increase in the "reliability" factor. If people can find you and your book on the internet, they will look more favorably at buying your book. If you leave your books on Amazon and let them handle the downloading and sales of your book, you don't need a website that handles ecommerce, just one that displays your name and that of your book and tells a little about each.

The customer downloading your ebook from the website to the his/her computer is using bandwidth; the more down-loads, the more the bandwidth usage. Some web hosts charge you extra for bandwidth usage beyond a certain point. So, if all of your books are "sold" by another entity, like Ama-zon, you don't need an commerce site, simply one that shows your picture and information and a picture of your book and information about it.

But, you DO need something to pique the customer's atten-tion, something to help them draw a connection to you, a "place" where they can go to look up your name and get that warm and fuzzy feeling necessary to get them to part with the price of your book.

bluehost.com and hostgator.com are two of the cheaper **web hosts** out there. But that does NOT mean they are cheaply put together! I use Hostgator because (1)it is one of the cheaper ones, but (2)it has more "stuff" that comes free than Go Daddy gives. Go Daddy is a wonderful web host, but they will nickel and dime you to DEATH, charging for every little thing that they think you might want! At least some of the cheaper web hosts have offerings in packages so that you're not paying extra for everything else, like mailboxes, and security, etc. If you want to compare many sites, go to Google, to the search bar, and plug in "best web hosts" or "cheap web hosts" and you get gazillions of suggestions. But look for one that says "10 Best Web Hosts" or "10 Cheapest Web Hosts." That will bring you to a comparison of 10 different sites.

Good Luck choosing one that will meet all of your needs without breaking your bank! See Appendix VI for additional web hosts that might serve your needs.

SEO

In addition to putting your books on various sales sites, you need to have your "keywords" honed. Keywords are the words or phrases that people put into the search bar on any search engine (like Google) to find your book or information about your book. It's a huge guessing game, on your part, to try and guess what phrase or word someone will enter in the search bar on Google, to look for a book like yours. If they have the exact title, great, the search engine will find it. If not, the chances of them finding your book just by the keywords they enter is only enhanced by "enhancing" your site keywords. This process is called Search Engine Optimization or SEO.

It's not a difficult process, but it *is* squirrely. Just when you think you've got a handle on what words are the best ones to use to get a higher ranking on the sales page, Google and the other search engines change the algorithms that pull your book up from the depths and your book starts floundering on the search pages. So, you have to use keywords that most people will enter WITHOUT using the ones that EVERY-BODY enters. Using the most common keywords means that your book's description may be WAY down toward oblivion rather than on the first page of search returns. Anything past the first page is usually not seen by the searcher.

There are numerous sites and SEO sites out there that will give you help in the direction of optimizing your website and your books on a sales site's sales page. Just plug in "SEO" or "Search Engine Optimization" or "keyword enhancement" or "keyword optimization" in the search bar. Then sift through and see what information you can find for free. There are DOZENS of options, people who claim to have "figured out" the perfect way to make your website better than most at gleaning through the paying customers and placing them at your door, and they'll charge you a pretty penny for that information. A few that might be helpful can be found on Appendix VII.

That about covers all the bases left in my memory. Just re-member. You are the authority on your subject (unless you are plagiarizing someone else's work!) and on the situation within your household. Only you know if you can afford to BUY some serious advertising, agenting, and publicity help or if you are going to have to "fake it until you make it," as I did!

Either way, Best Wishes in your endeavors!!

~~~~~~~~~~~~~~~~~~~~

Please feel free to contact me at johnnie.lewis@comcast.net, keeping in mind three things:

- I will NOT publish your book for you. I have too many brothers and a Better Half who are all aspiring authors and they take up all of my non-writing time…, along with my grandchildren!
- If your book doesn't sell on one marketplace, try changing the price, cover, or the marketplace.
- Your website reflects you! Change the opening screen every six months to something "new" and "different"!

GLOSSARY

BARCODE — A group of thick and thin lines that is placed on a product so that a computer can obtain the price of the product and other information about the product.

BRICK-AND-MORTAR-PUBLISHER — A publishing company that has a physical presence in the marketplace, with a building and other tangible properties, where one may go see an employee there.

"ELEVATOR SPEECH" — A 10-15 second speech that one can espouse, memorized, that gives information to an interested party. It may be information about one's self, family, book, car, etc. Called Elevator Speech because it's the shorter version of what you might tell your listener over coffee, but since you may not have but 10-15 seconds to impress or depress your listener, the information has to be shorter, with more "punch" to grab the listener's attention.

ISBN — International Standard Book Number. Required on most books, CDs, DVDs, etc. that will be sold in physical and online stores. Used in conjunction with a bar code.

MARKETPLACES — Physical or online stores or other sales places. Point of purchase locations where a customer can buy things. Ex: a service station is a marketplace for selling gasoline and other automobile necessities.

PERMABOUND — A method of binding a book that involves gluing the cover to the pages, then crimping the entire spine of the book very tightly in a vise.

PIPELINE — In business, the pipeline is the length of time in a product's life cycle from raw material to the shelves at the marketplace.

PRINT-ON-DEMAND — POD is a situation where a book, CD, etc. is not actually printed until a customer places an order for it at a marketplace outlet. When the order is placed and processed to the printer, the printer (or duplicating company) prints only the number of books ordered, then ships them to the customer with the marketplace's name on the shipping label. The action is transparent to the customer. It looks to the customer as if the book, etc. came directly from the marketplace.

SADDLE-STITCHED — A method of binding a book to hold the pages and cover together. Either the printer uses staples to hold the pages together (in the middle of the book) or uses stitches on the left outside edge of the book, stitching through the book from front to back, down the length of the book. Over this stitching is placed the cover, so that the stitching is not seen.

SEO — Search Engine Optimization is used to enhance an entry's place in a search engine toward the top of the list for the searched keyword. When a given keyword or phrase is entered in the Search Engine's (say, Google) search bar, a list of possible choices for the user to access will appear. SEO involves trying to find the most optimal keyword or combinations of keywords to get YOUR entry to the top of the list.

SLUSHPILE — The stack of large envelopes containing solicited or unsolicited manuscripts from potential authors, unopened and unread, sitting in the corner of an editor's office. An editor may not get to the bottom of that slush pile to get YOUR submission during his/her time on the job!

THUMB DRIVE — A flash drive, jazz drive or other term for a USB ported portable "memory stick" for retrieving and holding files to or from one computer to another.

WEB HOST — A company that provides space on servers for individuals or companies to buy/rent and use to promote their websites through.

APPENDIX I — Book Cover Designs

bookcoverarchive.com
fiverr.com/ebook_cover
bespokebookcovers.com
99designs.com
bookcoverarchive.com
thecreativepenn.com/bookcoverdesign/
coverdesignstudio.com
killercovers.com
okaycreations.com
gimp.com
createspace.com/tools/covercreator.jsp

A book cover being "glued" over the hardcover backing of a book. The "overlaps" are why the formatting for the hardcover must be larger than the finished book will be.

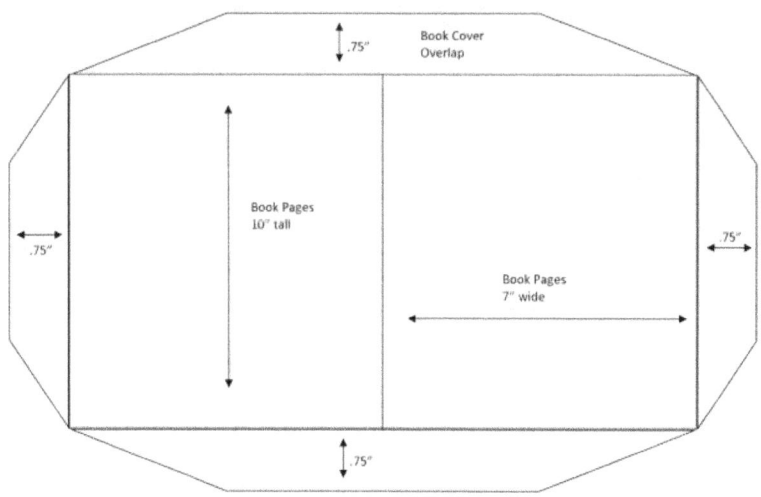

APPENDIX II — Sample Title and Copyright Pages

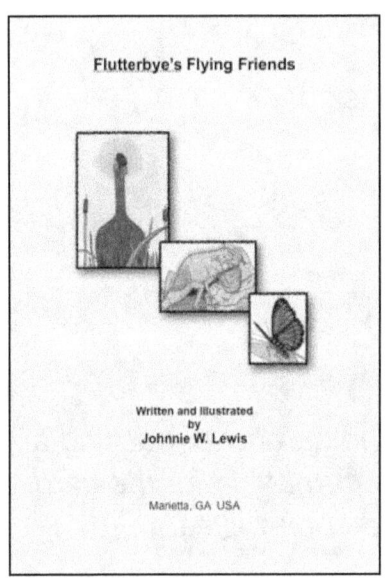

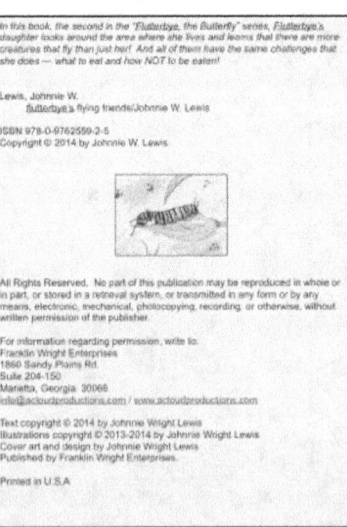

APPENDIX III — Audio/Video Recordings

Audio Recordings
acx.com (Amazon; for the DIY Section, skip down, on Home screen, to "Authors as Narrators" and watch the video)

wikihow.com/create-an-audiobook

makeuseof.com/tag/how-to-record-your-own-audiobook/

theatlantic.com/entertainment/archive/2013/08/the-unexpected-agony-of-recording-your-own-audiobook/278957/

lulu.com/blog/2012/11/audiobooks/

Look on amazon.com for *How to Create an Audiobook for Audible* for $0.99. Good book full of good information!

Video Recordings

camstudio.org (Open Source [free] program)

techsmith.com/camtasia.html (How to use Camtasia program)

nchsoftware.com/capture/

http://download.cnet.com/windows/video-capture-software/ (for Windows)

fraps.com

camtasia-studio.downloadable.co

APPENDIX IV — Resources

writersdigest.com

createspace.com

lightningsource.com

Building Your Book for Kindle (FREE ebook from Amazon)

How I Sold 1 Million eBooks in 5 Months! by John Locke ($2.99 ebook from Amazon; and any other ebooks in the "under $5 range" that tell how the author sold more books on Amazon are also good resources)

bookow.com/resources.php

amazon.com

bn.com

bowker.com

kunaki.com

APPENDIX V — Vanity Presses

American Biographical Institute
AuthorHouse
Books LLC
BiblioBazaar
Blurb, Inc.
Bob Books
CafePress
CreateSpace
Famous Poets Society
iUniverse
Kobo Writing Life
Lightning Source
Lulu
Notion Press
Outskirts Press
Poetry.com (also known as the International Library of
        Poetry)
PublishAmerica
Smashwords
Tate Publishing & Enterprises
Trafford Publishing
Vantage Press
Xlibris
Xulon Press
Wattpad

As you can see, many of the sources that I have espoused are listed here as vanity presses, though mine don't require payment up front. *Caveat Emptor.*

APPENDIX VI — Web Hosts

ipage.com

bluehost.com

hostgator.com

justhost.com

ipower.com

ixwebhosting.com

startlogic.com

1and1.com

web.com

I personally have used ipower.com and hostgator.com. Both are very good companies.

APPENDIX VII — Keyword Optimization

http://searchenginewatch.com/article/2303494/21-Best-FREE-SEO-Tools-for-On-Page-Optimization (article with a lot of free suggestions)

tools.seobook.com/keyword-list/generator.php

wordstream.com/blogs/ws/2010/04/14/keyword-optimization (article that gives an EXCELLENT explanation of *what* keywords are and *why* they are important)

orangesoda.com

moz.com

my.wordtracker.com

https://adwords.google.com/KeywordPlanner